THE B!G QUEST

PRESENTS

WHAT DOES IT TAKE TO BE AN EFFECTIVE LEADER?

A LEADERS GUIDE TO EFFECTIVENESS

FEATURING - DAVID PAPPOE JR.

The Big Question™

What makes a leader effective?

Published by Adventurous Publishing
Copyright © 2024 David Pappoe Jr.

Paperback ISBN: 978-1-913310-81-3
Hardback ISBN: 978-1-913310-80-6

Welcome to this edition on

Effective Leadership

DAVID PAPPOE Jr.

Ft DAVID PAPPOE Jr.

CEO of Energas west Africa limited & President at African energy chambers, Ghana.

energas.co.za

CONTENTS

DAVID PAPPOE Jr.

OUR
WHY

The Big Question is a brand that delve's deep into the minds of influential leaders and uncover their strategies through asking Big questions.

We believe that the journey from aspiration to achievement is both fascinating and instructive.

By asking leaders profound questions about their experiences, we gain valuable insights that can guide you in turning your own dreams into tangible outcomes.

In this book, we speak to David Pappoe Jr., the President of the African Energy Chamber in Ghana and Chief Executive Officer at Energas West Africa Limited.

He'll share his insights on Effective leadership, and what it truly takes to make a big impact.

Best,

-TBQ

INTRODUCTION

"THE BEST WAY TO PREDICT THE FUTURE IS TO CREATE IT."

-ABRAHAM LINCON

Leadership is an ancient and universal concept, deeply embedded in the very fabric of human society.

From the earliest days of our existence, in every team, family, or workplace, there has always been someone who steps up to lead. This phenomenon is not random —it is a manifestation of natural laws that dictate the dynamics of human interaction.

Certain individuals possess an innate ability to guide others, to bring order to chaos, and to inspire collective action. These natural-born leaders emerge not because of titles or positions, but because of a fundamental truth: leadership is about influence, vision, and the ability to inspire.

Have you ever wondered how another person just like yourself could have the wisdom and strategic intelligence to be superior to others?

How did certain individuals rise to guide others through triumphs and challenges?

Leadership didn't simply appear—it evolved over centuries, shaped by the needs of early societies, people and the wisdom of philosophers.

Let us find out how.

PART 1

A LEADERS *JOURNEY*

Throughout history, these leaders have risen to the forefront, whether in ancient tribal societies, where the strongest or wisest guided their communities, or in modern organizations, where individuals with a unique blend of talent and charisma naturally step into leadership roles.

This tendency for leadership to emerge from within any group is a testament to the natural laws that govern human behavior. When faced with challenges, people instinctively look to those who demonstrate confidence, decisiveness, and the ability to navigate uncertainty. It is these qualities that mark the true leader, one who steps up not out of a desire for power, but out of a sense of responsibility and purpose.

But leadership, in its simplest form, is not always synonymous with effective leadership. This distinction is critical and often overlooked.

Leading vs. Effective Leadership

At its core, leading is about taking charge, directing others, and making decisions. It is the act of stepping up when guidance is needed, whether in a moment of crisis or during routine operations.

Anyone can lead by making decisions or issuing commands, but leading alone does not guarantee success. Leadership, in this basic sense, is about being in front—setting a direction and expecting others to follow.

However, effective leadership goes beyond mere direction. It is about achieving results, inspiring others, and creating an environment where individuals can thrive and contribute to a shared vision.

Effective leadership is characterized by a deep understanding of the people being led, clear communication and emotional intelligence.

PART 2

A HISTORY OF
EMOTIONAL INTELLIGENCE

Emotional intelligence (EI) is the ability to understand and manage your own emotions while also recognizing and influencing the emotions of others. This concept, brought to the forefront by psychologist Daniel Goleman in the 1990s, is now recognized as a critical component of effective leadership.

Unlike traditional intelligence (IQ), which measures cognitive abilities, emotional intelligence encompasses skills related to emotional awareness, self-regulation, empathy, and social interaction.

In the early days of psychological research, the focus was primarily on cognitive intelligence (IQ) as the key determinant of leadership potential and success. However, as researchers like Goleman and others began to study the factors that truly differentiated effective leaders from others, it became clear that emotional intelligence played a significant role.

Early studies and experiments in the 20th century, such as those conducted by psychologist Edward Thorndike on social intelligence, laid the groundwork for understanding how emotional and social competencies contribute to leadership effectiveness.

These tests showed that leaders who could empathize with their team members, manage their own emotions, and navigate social complexities were more successful in leading teams and organizations.

The shift from prioritizing IQ to incorporating emotional intelligence marked a significant evolution in leadership theory. Today, emotional intelligence is considered as important, if not more so, than cognitive abilities in determining a leader's effectiveness.

PART 3

DAVID PAPPOE Jr.

THE ART OF
EFFECTIVE LEADERSHIP

While anyone can assume the role of a leader, an effective leader creates positive outcomes, fosters collaboration, and builds trust. Effective leadership involves not just issuing orders, but listening, mentoring, and providing the resources and support necessary for the team to succeed.

The art of effective leadership is creating a culture of accountability and continuous improvement, where each member of the team feels valued and is encouraged to reach their full potential.

In my journey, from the corporate world to entrepreneurship and leadership within Ghana's energy sector, I have encountered both types of leadership. Early in my career, I witnessed leaders who were quick to take charge but lacked the ability to connect with their teams or achieve sustainable results.

These experiences taught me that true leadership effectiveness comes from more than just holding a position of authority; it requires a commitment to personal growth, strategic thinking, and a genuine concern for the well-being of others.

As you navigate your own path, whether in business, community work, or any other field, remember that the goal is not just to lead but to lead effectively. This means focusing not just on where you want to go, but on how you get there and who you bring along with you.

Leadership is a journey, and effective leadership is the compass that ensures you reach your destination with integrity and success.

From the tribal chieftains of ancient civilizations to the visionary entrepreneurs of today, leadership has always been about more than just authority—it's about influence, vision, and the ability to inspire. But not all leaders have succeeded in these roles.

History is also littered with examples of ineffective leaders whose poor decisions led to disastrous outcomes.

The concept of leadership is as old as humanity itself. In the earliest human societies, leaders emerged out of necessity.

They were often the strongest or the wisest, responsible for making decisions that affected the entire group— whether it was where to hunt, how to protect the tribe, or how to resolve conflicts. Leadership in these contexts was about survival. The role of the leader was to guide, protect, and provide for their people.

As societies evolved, so did the nature of leadership. In ancient civilizations like Egypt and Mesopotamia, leaders were often seen as divine or semi-divine figures,

entrusted not only with governance but with maintaining cosmic order. In ancient Greece, the concept of leadership began to incorporate more democratic ideals, particularly in city-states like Athens, where leaders were chosen by the people and were expected to govern with their consent.

A HISTORY OF
LEADERS

My own journey into leadership began in 2008 when I was working at a bank in Ghana. Initially, my role was to handle international transfers in the foreign department.

However, my versatility soon became apparent, and I found myself handling various roles across the bank. This experience taught me an important lesson: leadership is not just about the position you hold, but about how you adapt to challenges and seize opportunities.

One day, the managing director told me something that changed my life: "I hope you won't waste your talent working for others. You have potential that needs to be harnessed independently."

This statement resonated deeply with me, setting me on the path toward entrepreneurship. I realized that true leadership often involves taking risks, stepping out of your comfort zone, and pursuing a vision that others may not yet see.

And it made me ponder why people with incredible talents work for others.

As my journey continued, I found myself stepping into a new and challenging role within Ghana's energy sector. In recent years, I became the President of the African Energy Chamber (AEC) in Ghana, a position that has allowed me to contribute significantly to the development of our nation's energy resources.

With over 13 years of experience in the hydrocarbon industry, I have focused on promoting local content in the energy sector, which is crucial for driving socioeconomic development in Ghana and across Africa.

In addition to my role with the AEC, I serve as the
Executive Director of Energas West Africa Limited, an
engineering and energy services firm. Through this
role, I contribute to maximizing upstream, midstream,
and downstream activities for various projects by
providing turnkey engineering and consulting services.

I also represent Petrographics, an Egyptian oil services
company in Ghana, where I am involved in workforce
development and the training of geologists and other
technical personnel.

This leadership role in the energy sector has been a natural extension of my entrepreneurial journey, allowing me to blend my business acumen with a strong commitment to national development.

The energy sector is a critical component of Ghana's future, and I am proud to play a part in shaping policies and discussions around local content, ensuring that our nation and its people can benefit fully from our natural resources.

Throughout history, some of the most influential leaders have been military commanders. Figures like Alexander the Great, Julius Caesar, and Genghis Khan reshaped the world through their conquests. Their leadership was characterized by strategic brilliance, charismatic authority, and the ability to inspire loyalty among their troops.

However, their legacies were not without controversy. Their empires often expanded at the cost of immense human suffering, teaching us that the consequences of leadership are as important as its achievements.

In my own career, I've drawn lessons from military leaders, particularly their focus on strategy and their ability to adapt to changing circumstances. When I later moved to Silverstar, the company representing Mercedes-Benz in Ghana, my goal was clear: to build a network with high-net-worth individuals.

Selling luxury cars wasn't just a job—it was a strategic move to position myself among the elite, to learn from them, and to understand what made them successful.

Religious leaders have also played pivotal roles in history. Figures like Moses, Jesus Christ, the Prophet Muhammad, and the Buddha have influenced not just their followers but entire civilizations.

Their leadership was based on spiritual authority and moral guidance. They were able to inspire people to follow a path of righteousness, often in the face of great adversity.

With the rise of nation-states, leadership became more formalised. Monarchs, presidents, and prime ministers emerged as central figures in governance, responsible for creating laws, enforcing order, and representing their nations on the world stage.

The nature of political leadership has varied greatly, but the best political leaders have always understood that power comes with immense responsibility.

In my own leadership roles, whether in business or community initiatives, I've been mindful of the responsibility that comes with leadership. Effective leaders understand that their decisions have far-reaching consequences, not just for themselves but for everyone they lead.

This is why I've always strived to lead by example, demonstrating integrity, accountability, and professionalism in everything I do.

While history is full of examples of great leaders, it's also replete with examples of ineffective leadership. Leaders who lack vision, fail to communicate effectively, or govern with selfish motives can cause significant harm. Consider leaders like King Louis XVI of France, whose inability to address the financial crises and social unrest led to the French Revolution and the fall of the monarchy.

Or more extreme cases, like Adolf Hitler and Joseph Stalin, whose leadership resulted in immense suffering and loss of life.

In the energy sector, ineffective leadership can result in the mismanagement of resources, environmental degradation, and the disenfranchisement of local communities.

This is why my work with the AEC is focused not just on exploiting energy resources but on doing so in a way that is ethical, sustainable, and beneficial to the broader population.

These examples serve as powerful reminders of the damage that poor leadership can do. In my own experience, I've seen how ineffective leadership can erode trust, stifle innovation, and lead to failure.

That's why I believe so strongly in the importance of effective communication, strategic thinking, and moral integrity as the pillars of good leadership.

In today's world, leadership is more complex than ever. Globalization, technological advancements, and social media have changed the way leaders interact with their followers and the world.

Leaders today must navigate a rapidly changing landscape, balancing the needs of their constituents with the demands of a globalized economy and the challenges of climate change, inequality, and geopolitical tensions.

As I continue my entrepreneurial journey, I've found that modern leadership requires a commitment to continuous learning and adaptation. The world is changing at an unprecedented pace, and leaders must be willing to evolve with it.

This means staying informed about global trends, being open to new ideas, and constantly seeking ways to improve both personally and professionally.

The history of leadership is a story of individuals who have shaped the course of human events, for better or worse.

From the earliest tribal chieftains to the leaders of modern nation-states and social movements, leadership has been about more than just holding power. It is about guiding others, making tough decisions, and inspiring change.

As I reflect on my own journey, I realize that the lessons of history are as relevant today as they have ever been.

Whether you're leading a nation, a business, or a community, the principles of effective leadership remain the same: communicate clearly, act with integrity, and always strive to make a positive impact. As we move forward, the world will continue to need leaders who can rise to the challenges of their time— leaders who can inspire, innovate, and guide humanity toward a better future.

Entrepreneurship is far from easy. There are days when everything goes wrong, and times when giving up seems tempting. I've experienced these moments firsthand.

At one point, my business wasn't performing as expected, and I lost a significant amount of money. Leaving me feeling defeated.

But these challenges taught me the true meaning of leadership.

I learned to step back, analyze the situation, and address problems methodically. Instead of letting adversity defeat me, I used it as fuel to push forward. Re-strategizing and bringing in smarter people to help find solutions is crucial. Surround yourself with a team that believes in your vision, and give them the tools to succeed. Together, you can overcome any obstacle.

While effective leadership can lead to growth and success, ineffective leadership can cause untold damage. History offers countless examples of leaders whose poor decisions resulted in catastrophic outcomes.

At the same time, the core principles of leadership—integrity, vision, and empathy—will remain as important as ever.

These are the qualities that will enable us to navigate the challenges ahead and build businesses that are not only successful but also meaningful and impactful.

MY BIG QUESTION TO YOU THE READER, IS

WHAT'S HOLDING YOU BACK?

ABOUT THE *AUTHOR*

David Pappoe Jr. is a prominent figure in Africa's energy sector, serving as the President of the African Energy Chamber (AEC) in Ghana. With over 13 years of experience in the hydrocarbon industry, Pappoe is a key advocate for the full exploitation of Africa's oil and gas resources to combat energy poverty.

He is instrumental in shaping local content and workforce development across the continent.

In addition to his role at the AEC, Pappoe is the country representative for Petrographics, an Egyptian Oil Services Company, and the Executive Director of Energas West Africa Limited. His work involves driving upstream, midstream, and downstream activities, as well as training geologists and other specialists in reservoir development and management.

Pappoe's efforts focus on fostering partnerships between African and European firms, particularly in the oil and gas sector, and promoting socioeconomic development through local content prioritization.

David Pappoe Jr. (*2nd to the left*) with NJ Ayuk (*to the closest right of David*) and friends at the African Energy Chambers Oil Summit.

David (*far right*) speaking at football legend Clarence seedorf's *Black Impact foundation* summit (*BIF*) in dubai 2024 on the future of oil and gas in africa.

With Paolo - founder and CEO of TBQ (left) and Amire Ben
salmi (middle) in dubai.

The African Energy Chamber (AEC) is the leading voice of the African energy sector, dedicated to promoting investment and private sector participation across the continent's oil, gas, and renewable energy industries. Founded by NJ Ayuk, the AEC advocates for the sustainable development of Africa's energy resources to drive economic growth and alleviate energy poverty.

The Chamber focuses on creating opportunities for local content development, fostering partnerships between African and international companies, and ensuring that Africa's energy potential benefits its people.

Scan the QR on the next page to find out more.

Be you,
be bold,
Go big.

-TBQ

NOTES

THE B!G QUESTION.

_____
_____
_____
_____
_____
_____
_____
_____
_____
_____
_____
_____
_____
_____
_____
_____
_____
_____
_____
_____
_____...........GO B!G

THE B!G QUESTION.

_____
_____
_____
_____
_____
_____
_____
_____
_____
_____
_____
_____
_____
_____
_____
_____
_____
_____
_____............GO B!G

THE B!G QUESTION.

_____
_____
_____
_____
_____
_____
_____
_____
_____
_____
_____
_____
_____
_____
_____
_____
_____
_____
_____...........GO B!G

THE B!G QUESTION.

_____
_____
_____
_____
_____
_____
_____
_____
_____
_____
_____
_____
_____
_____
_____
_____
_____
_____
_____............GO B!G

THE B!G QUESTION.

_____
_____
_____
_____
_____
_____
_____
_____
_____
_____
_____
_____
_____
_____
_____
_____
_____

............GO B!G

THE B!G QUESTION.

_____

_____

_____

_____

_____

_____

_____

_____

_____

_____

_____

_____

_____

_____

_____

_____

_____.............GO B!G

THE B!G QUESTION.

_____

_____

_____

_____

_____

_____

_____

_____

_____

_____

_____

_____

_____

...........GO B!G

THE B!G QUESTION.

_____
_____
_____
_____
_____
_____
_____
_____
_____
_____
_____
_____
_____
_____
_____
_____
_____
_____
_____...........GO B!G

THE B!G QUESTION.

_____

_____

_____

_____

_____

_____

_____

_____

_____

_____

_____

_____

_____

_____

_____

_____

_____

............GO B!G

THE B!G QUESTION.

_____
_____
_____
_____
_____
_____
_____
_____
_____
_____
_____
_____
_____
_____
_____
_____
_____
_____
_____............GO B!G

THE B!G QUESTION.

_____
_____
_____
_____
_____
_____
_____
_____
_____
_____
_____
_____
_____
_____
_____
_____
_____
_____............GO B!G

THE B!G QUESTION.

_____
_____
_____
_____
_____
_____
_____
_____
_____
_____
_____
_____
_____
_____
_____
_____
_____
_____...........GO B!G

THE B!G QUESTION.

..............GO B!G

THE B!G QUESTION.

_____
_____
_____
_____
_____
_____
_____
_____
_____
_____
_____
_____
_____
_____
_____
_____
_____
_____
_____
_____............GO B!G

THE B!G QUESTION.

_____
_____
_____
_____
_____
_____
_____
_____
_____
_____
_____
_____
_____
_____
_____
_____
_____
_____
_____......GO B!G

THE B!G QUESTION.

_____

_____

_____

_____

_____

_____

_____

_____

_____

_____

_____

_____

_____

_____

_____

_____

_____

_____

_____

_____...........GO B!G

THE B!G QUESTION.

_____
_____
_____
_____
_____
_____
_____
_____
_____
_____
_____
_____
_____
_____
_____
............GO B!G
_____

THE B!G QUESTION.

_____
_____
_____
_____
_____
_____
_____
_____
_____
_____
_____
_____
_____
_____
_____
_____
_____
_____.............GO B!G

THE B!G QUESTION.

..............GO B!G

THE B!G QUESTION.

_____
_____
_____
_____
_____
_____
_____
_____
_____
_____
_____
_____
_____
_____
_____
_____
_____
_____
_____............GO B!G

in **The Big Question**

⊙ @thebigquestionhq

✉ thebigquestioninfo@gmail.com

99
GO B!G...

www.ingramcontent.com/pod-product-compliance
Lightning Source LLC
Chambersburg PA
CBHW060635210326
41520CB00010B/1613